D0331046

To: Laura
From: Joyce
Xmas 1991

Clarkson Potter / Publishers
New York 1991

# A

# PERFECTLY
# IRREGULAR
# CHRISTMAS
# TREE

Written & Illustrated by Abbie Zabar

"Rockefeller Center"
is a registered service mark of The Rockefeller Group.

Published by Clarkson N. Potter, Inc.
201 East 50th Street, New York, New York 10022.
Member of the Crown Publishing Group.

CLARKSON N. POTTER, POTTER and Colophon are trademarks of
Clarkson N. Potter, Inc.

Manufactured in Japan

Library of Congress Cataloging-in-Publication Data
Zabar, Abbie
A perfectly irregular Christmas tree / Abbie Zabar
p. cm.
1. Christmas Trees -- Poetry          I. Title
PS3576. A14P47    1991              91-11196
811'.54 -- dc20                        CIP

ISBN 0-517-58608-8

10 9 8 7 6 5 4 3 2 1

First Edition

to the irregularities in life

I

There is a farm where Christmas trees grow
deep in a valley, dappled with snow.

Acres and acres of chubby little trees
grow to attention like green tepees
because row after row after row after row
were planted and pruned by the farmer John Doe.

Throughout winter, even early as fall,
when other limbs wear no leaves at all,
these remain forever green,
seeming fluffy and soft as velveteen.

But nature being somewhat tricky
made their needles sharp and sticky.
So whether in storms or a flurry
a balsam fir might look rather furry.

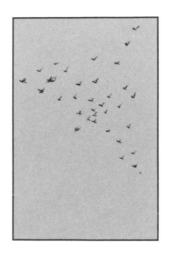

The time of year came
when snow replaced rain,
when songbirds went south,
when deer jutted out.

When firewood smoke scented the air,
when skiers donned long underwear,
when sand flies and seedpods all blew away,
when nighttime lasted longer than day.

When bears went off to hibernate,
when kids came home to celebrate,
when September, October, and November had passed,
when in just a few weeks it'd be Christmas, at last.

**Ⅱ**

**A**ll over New York, turned festive and pretty,
trees were unloaded throughout the city.

Still many shoppers chose to pass
sidewalk selections roped en masse
because up in the country, covered with snow,
was a farm where Christmas trees glow.

Then one year, an odd seedling started to grow.
Smack in the middle, it seemed to self-sow.
And though it had an unusual sheen
the little blue spruce wished to be green.

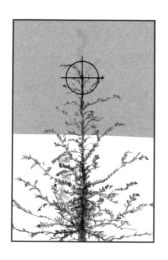

What's more, several hunters without any heart
made the top a shooter's mark
So even with its lovely scent
folks only saw a point that was bent.

Suddenly, within a week,
the landscape turned quite bleak.
The ground grew bare.
No Christmas trees were left anywhere.

Quickly cut down and sold,
they all turned into farmer's gold.
Every tree was taken away
to decorate a home on Christmas day.

All except for the sad-hearted spruce.
Again and again it was of no use.
Flat on one side and not quite green,
how could it make the big city scene?

nother year had come and gone
leaving the Spruce alone on the farm

But construction work begun in the summer
was about to make this season a bummer.
Building scaffolds in Rockefeller Center
would still be up through December.

Grim headlines in every newspaper
mourned the unadorned skyscraper.
For the first time in memory,
ROCKEFELLER CENTER'S GOT NO CHRISTMAS TREE!

It seems the tree planned for the site,
though perfect around, just wasn't right.
Too fluffy and puffy, and a real pushover,
it kept falling down on Prometheus' shoulder.

(Poor Prometheus. The needles sure hurt
and how he longed for an old T-shirt.)

The Big Boss, not knowing what to do,
fearing this could be his Waterloo,
drove to the country all covered with snow,
Pining away for Christmas-tree glow.

Down in the valley, where they had grown,
stood a crooked spruce totally alone.
Indeed this one had a peculiar shape,
even more pronounced in a white landscape.

It certainly cast an odd silhouette,
the kind most folks would rather forget,
but if the branches hid birds like under a wing,
could it do the same for scaffolding?

IV

Time was of the essence.
Crowds gathered 'round in suspense.

The spruce got hoisted into place.
Suddenly, rusty pipes were cloaked in delicate grace,
candelabra arms went upside down, inside out,
camouflaging ugly scaffolds all about.

Across the city they shouted Hooray!
The Scraggly tree had saved the day.
Everyone nodded Congratulations.
Wait! What about the decorations?

Too late. Yet no one was dissatisfied,
and the weeping spruce filled with pride.
Never dreaming it could bring such bliss,
the blue tree cried and cried from happiness.

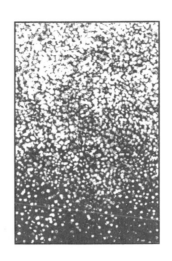

Then after midnight came the snow.
Temperatures dropped to below zero.
Frozen tears hung from every limb
decking branches with icicle trim.

But Christmas day was sunny and bright
and the Spruce turned silver in morning light.
So what might have once seemed an irregular tree
Came to the rescue perfectly.

The End

# POSTSCRIPT

Six weeks before Christmas and still before dawn, a timber truck transports a well-corseted, tarp-covered bundle into midtown Manhattan. There is an escort of police cars and all traffic signals have been synchronized along a designated route. ✳ Standard operating procedure for any visiting V.I.P.

Riggers and heavy-lift equipment are on site before 8 A.M. And by noon the multistoried crane has hoisted aloft a monumental tree, setting it upright on a massive platform, where it will be anchored 'til after the new year. Then, over the course of a week, carpenters will work on 8 levels of pipe-and-plank staging, repairing any broken limbs, as 25 electricians haul 20,000 lights strung on miles of wire to trim the towering evergreen that rises above the giant gold-leafed statue ✳ Once again, Prometheus assumes his holiday role as guardian of New York City's most illustrious seasonal symbol.

What is now venerable tradition has come a long way since 1931 when a tinsel-decorated balsam graced the muddy Rockefeller Center excavation site. Yet to workers lined up waiting to receive their paychecks on a Depression-era Christmas Eve, no tree ever looked better. ✳ Its spritely green branches celebrated Christmas as well as the indomitable human spirit.

Every year since 1971 Rockefeller Center's Christmas tree has been chipped for mulch. ✳ Recycled and returned to the earth.

>≫< Thank You >≫<

Roy Finamore.
Howard Klein, Anne-Marie Colban,
Mary Albi, Alan Heller, Mary Flower,
Yolanda Beltran, James Reed, Carl Miller,
Joy Sikorski, Ed Wilkin, Jerry Wilson &
Timothy!